How to be
a *great* godparent

Your guide to fulfilling
a wonderful role

Susan Hardwick

First published in 2003 by

KEVIN MAYHEW LTD
Buxhall, Stowmarket, Suffolk, IP14 3BW
E-mail: info@kevinmayhewltd.com

KINGSGATE PUBLISHING INC
1000 Pannell Street, Suite G, Columbia, MO 65201
E-mail: sales@kingsgatepublishing.com

9 8 7 6 5 4 3 2 1 0

ISBN 1 84417 152 3
Catalogue No 1500638

Cover design by Angela Selfe
Edited by Graham Harris
Typesetting by Richard Weaver

Printed and bound in Great Britain

Introduction

I was really pleased to be asked to write this booklet, since I have godchildren whose ages range from 6 to late 30s.

It is a great compliment when a parent asks you to be a god-parent, but individual motivations vary widely. It is often a mixture of all three of the following reasons:

- The child's parents might want to indicate the affection and high esteem in which they hold you.

- If anything were to happen to them as parents they might want you to ensure that there is a safe and secure haven for their child.

- They could also be choosing you as the person who they feel will best provide religious, spiritual and emotional support for their child.

This booklet sets out what being a godparent entails. It also makes some suggestions about how to be the sort of godparent who makes a real difference to the life and well-being of your godchild.

Susan Hardwick

> . . . I will sprinkle
> clean water over you
> and you shall be cleansed . . .
>
> I will give you a new heart
> and put a new spirit
> within you . . .
>
> Ezekiel 36:25a, 26

My godchild ....

Birthday

....

Parents

....

....

Baptised

On ....

At ....

....

Place picture of your
godchild here

Special memories of the day

....

....

....

What infant baptism is and what it entails

The dictionary definition of a godparent paints an untaxing image: 'A person who presents a child at baptism and responds on the child's behalf.'

And it's true, your first role to fulfil as a godparent is a practical one, in keeping with that dictionary definition. At the baptism or christening service you will join with the other godparents and the child's parents making promises on the infant's behalf. As godparent you will also promise to ensure that the child is taught the Christian faith, and to encourage him/her to come to Confirmation at the appropriate time, where the child can make the baptism promises for him/herself. And there, for many people, the responsibility ends.

But there can be so very much more. It can be the beginning of a childhood-long, maybe even lifelong, relationship and responsibility. The church expectation of a godparent is, not surprisingly, rather fuller than the dictionary definition. Christening – or baptism, as it is always called in the Bible – is, literally, a Christ-ing. It is 'becoming Christ's'. It is a ceremony of beginning or becoming. When a person experiences the waters of baptism, (s)he begins a life belonging to Christ.

(S)he is no longer her or his own, but God's. The water symbolises the washing away of the old life. The person turns to Christ and asks him into her or his life. They can turn to the future, with the slate washed clean, assured that God walks with them – guiding, supporting and strengthening them.

Infant baptism or christening is the parents' way of acknowledging that their child is a gift from God and that they would like to dedicate their child to him. The parents might have a desire or even an expectation that their child will develop a relationship with God, so that they can decide whether to take their own decision about Confirmation and all that it entails.

So does infant baptism or christening make you a Christian?

Well, baptism is not magic, and God's love is not magically switched on by any earthly ritual; it is there anyway.

Baptism is an outward sign and symbol of an inward event. So for an adult there has to be faith and a real commitment to give their life to God.

For a small child this obviously cannot be a commitment that (s)he can make – which is why the parents and godparents do it on the child's behalf.

So what are the requirements? What is expected of you as a godparent?

The first thing to say is that this booklet is by no means an exhaustive reference book covering every facet of every denomination's interpretation or understanding of what a godparent should be.

Each set of parents will have different expectations of you, and each minister at each church will have different advice to impart as to how you can fulfil this role.

However, the basic fact remains consistent, irrespective of the denomination of the church at which you're performing your duties as godparents. The fact is that you are being asked to make promises in the sight of God and in his presence, so this role is not to be taken lightly.

Some ministers and some churches will expect godparents to have been baptised themselves, but even if you don't have any deep belief in God when you are invited to become a godparent, that might not necessarily preclude you from being one.

If that is your situation, discuss it when you meet the minister prior to the baptism or christening. Her or his hope will probably be that as you approach this task you will take note of all that is said at the service and, in accepting your role as godparent, it may be that you will want to explore and develop your own relationship with God.

In the beginning

Godparents are not, in fact, mentioned in the Bible, but they do appear in descriptions of infant baptisms in the early church. They are described as being alongside the parents, acting as proxies for the child being baptised.

Rituals of initiation, however, are mentioned in both the Old and the New Testaments. Abraham was initiated into the covenant of God *(Genesis 17)*. And John the Baptist preached a baptism of repentance, symbolised and expressed in baptism *(Luke 3)*. Jesus, it seems, took over baptism from John and commanded his disciples to continue this after his death. Proclamation of the Good News of Jesus Christ, and baptism, went together – one was the inward, and one was the outward. If you wanted to be treated as a believer, you had to be baptised – it was the sign of your conversion.

A living relationship with your godchild

- Be an ongoing presence in your godchild's life. Do not be a hit-and-run godparent, present at the baptism and from then on conspicuous by your absence. Just being around and being available is an important part of the role.

- Remember the anniversary of their baptism each year, with a gift of religious significance.

- Keep up with their changing needs and personalities and adapt your relationship accordingly, so that it remains relevant and appropriate.

- Pray for them regularly.

- Pray regularly for yourself, for your role as godparent.

- Try to set a good example.

- Be fun and interesting to know and to have as a godparent.

- Let them know often how much you care for them and how much you value being their godparent.

- Have real conversations with them about as wide a range of things as you can, so they really know you are interested and care about *all* aspects of their lives.

- If their relationship with their parents – or even their parents' relationship with each other – is under strain, a trusted, regularly present and readily available godparent can provide much-needed support and understanding. A godparent may even, on occasions, act as honest broker – for example, between rebellious teenager and despairing parent.

- At the appropriate time, probably early teens, you may wish to ask your godchild whether they had thought about Confirmation and making their baptism promises for themselves.

Some prayers and reflections

Regular prayers

SUNDAY

**My godchild's
spiritual life**

Jesus – May _____ grow in *his*
    knowledge and love of you each day.
May every step of *his* life be walked
    along your way.
Watch over *him* and guide *him*
to know you as *his* Lord and Saviour.
Amen.

MONDAY

**My godchild's
wisdom and
learning**

Heavenly Father – give _____
    a deep love of learning
and the wisdom to understand how to
    use the knowledge *she* gains.
May *she* know the joy of curiosity and
    wonder in your beautiful world.
May *she* never stop asking questions.
Amen.

TUESDAY

**My godchild's
happiness**

Lord of all – bless _____ with a
    deep sense of joy and happiness
    throughout *his* life.
When times are hard – as sometimes
    they will be – may *he* still have a
    thankful heart
for blessings received and for your
    faithful presence.
Amen.

WEDNESDAY

My godchild's relationships

Jesus – may _____ always know
   the joys of loving and being loved.
May *she* never know what it is to be
   lonely.
May *she* be generous and compassionate
and quick to understand and respond to
   the needs of others.
May the world be a better place for *her*
   presence.
Amen.

THURSDAY

My godchild's health

Lord of healing and wholeness – may
   your healing hand hover over
   _____ always
and keep *her* healthy and well.
May *her* body grow straight and strong.
May *her* mind be equally true.
Amen.

FRIDAY

My godchild's safety

Heavenly Father – watch over every
   step _____ takes.
Keep *him* safe.
Guard and protect *him.*
May nothing harm *him.*
May *he* be alert to danger of any kind
and wise as to what *he* should do.
Amen.

SATURDAY

My godchild's future

God of all – guide _____ along
the path of life you have chosen for *her*.
May *she* greet each bright new day
with joy and excitement
at all that it might bring.
May *she* always be filled with wonder.
May *she* always walk with you.
Amen.

Prayers for special times

The day of my godchild's baptism

Lord – walk with _____ and
guide *her*.
Watch over *her*. Keep *her* safe.
May all *her* days be filled with wonder
and joy
and with the nearness of you.
Amen.

Heavenly Father – this is such a
wondrous day in _____ 's life.
This is such a wondrous day in mine.
May it be the beginning of a lifelong
relationship of loving and caring
between us three:
he, me and you.
Amen.

Jesus – on _____ 's special day
there is so much I want to pray for.
My heart is brimming over with wishes
and hopes and dreams for *her*.
May those that are right for *her* come
true.

I'm filled with awe at all that it means
  to be *her* godparent.
Help me to do it as you would want.
Help me to be faithful to the promises I
  shall make.
Amen.

My godchild's birthday

Heavenly Father – on _____ 's
  birthday, I think back to the day of *his*
  birth
and give thanks for all the joy *he* has
  given since then.
May this year to come be filled with
  good things for *him* and a multitude
  of blessings.
Amen.

The anniversary of my godchild's baptism

Jesus – today is the anniversary of
  _____ 's baptism
and I hold *her* especially in my prayers.
May the blessings conferred that day
  continue to shape *her.*
May the memory of that day and the
  promises I made,
always remain fresh and sweet in my
  mind and heart.
Amen.

Prayers to keep coming back to . . .

My relationship with my godchild

Jesus – guide me through the days and
  years,
in my relationship with _____ .
May I always be sensitive and
  responsive to *his* needs.

Give me the wisdom and insight and
    awareness
as to what attitude and behaviour is
    appropriate and right.
May all that I do be pleasing to you.
Amen.

My responsibilities   Heavenly Father – I want to be a good
    godparent to _____
and I guess that will mean different
    things at different times.
Open my mind and my imagination to a
    wide understanding and appreciation
of what it is to be a good godparent.
    Then please help me to do it to the
    best of my ability.
Amen.

. . . and one for a very special occasion

My godchild's
Confirmation   Lord – I am so proud of _____
    and that *she* has chosen to be
    Confirmed.
I pray for *her* as *she* prepares to make
    the baptism promises for *her*self.
It is a moment of completion, as well as
    a new beginning.
Bless *her* commitment.
May *she* stay as faithful to you, as you
    have to *her*.
Amen.

What the Bible says

Jesus' ministry places great emphasis on children and their place in the kingdom of God.

Many verses in the Bible refer directly to their teaching and upbringing, and there is also guidance to parents or adults concerning their wider care.

These verses will help you to find out more of God's will for your godchild and to put in a biblical context the key part you can play in his or her life.

Old Testament

Exodus
14:19-31

Deuteronomy
30:15-20

Joshua
24:14-24

2 Kings
5:1-15a

Psalms
18:30-36; 25:1-10; 27:1-8;
34:1-8; 97:9-12; 107:1-9;
121

Isaiah
43:1-3a, 6, 7; 44:1-5

Jeremiah
31:31-34

Ezekiel
36:25a, 26-28

* Extra-special texts

New Testament

Matthew
3:11; 16:24-27; 28:16-20

Mark
1:1-11; 1:14-20

Luke
24:45-50

John
3:1-8; 14:15-18; 15:1-11

Acts
2:37-41*; 8:26-38; 16:25-34;
22:1-16

Romans
6:3-11*; 8:11-17; 10:9

1 Corinthians
12:12, 13

2 Corinthians
5:17*

Galatians
3:26, 27; 5:16-25

1 Peter
2:4-10; 3:21

Jesus came from Nazareth
in Galilee
and was baptised in the Jordan
by John . . .

Mark 1:9

. . . you are the children of God . . .
since every one of you
that has been baptised
has been clothed
in Christ.

Galatians 3:26a-27